Original title:
Spruce Up Your Sonnets

Copyright © 2025 Creative Arts Management OÜ
All rights reserved.

Author: Charles Whitfield
ISBN HARDBACK: 978-1-80567-205-0
ISBN PAPERBACK: 978-1-80567-504-4

Enhancing the Echo

In a world where rhymes collide,
Chasing words like a joyful ride.
Laughter dances on every page,
As we unleash the wit and sage.

Add a twist, a pun or two,
Words that giggle, words that woo.
Echoes bounce off every wall,
Making poetry an endless ball.

The Alchemy of Artful Arrangement

Stir the pot with a crafty line,
A sprinkle of humor makes it shine.
Transform the mundane into delight,
Watch your stanzas take flight.

Wit in words—a magic touch,
Turn plain prose into a crutch.
Arrange them like a jester's hat,
And see how laughter finds its chat.

A Revival of Romantic Rhythms

Love is silly, love is sweet,
With goofy verses on repeat.
Hearts are dancing, can you see?
Romance wears a clown's decree.

Sonnet spins on a merry-go,
With punchlines hidden just below.
A kiss is just a gentle nudge,
In this ballet, don't you budge!

Unfolding the Beauty of Language

Words unfurl like a flower's bloom,
Chasing joy, dispelling gloom.
Language flips like a tumbleweed,
Sprinkling fun in every deed.

Crafting verses with playful flair,
Banishing boredom from the air.
Sentences dance, they prance and spin,
A laughter fest where all can win.

Forest Hues: A Poetic Palette

In the heart of the woods, colors collide,
Green and brown in a merry ride.
Squirrels wear ties, while birds don hats,
Even the mushrooms dance with the cats.

Leaves chuckle softly, a rustling breeze,
Whispering secrets among the trees.
Nature's canvas, a playful show,
Painting giggles wherever we go.

Rhymes Beneath the Boughs

Underneath branches, a rhyme takes flight,
Frogs croak sonnets late in the night.
A bear takes notes, sits down with a sigh,
While owls roll their eyes at the sky.

Bumblebees buzz a light-hearted tune,
As daisies dance under the bright moon.
Crickets strum softly, a humorous play,
In this wild world, let laughter convey.

Sonnets from the Silent Woods

Among the trees, where silence reigns,
A poet trips over hidden gains.
Mice laugh hard at the awkward sight,
As branches lower, ready to bite.

Vines stretch out with a curious tug,
While pinecones giggle, snug as a bug.
Sonnets echo, in a quirky round,
Nature's laughter, the sweetest sound.

Rejuvenate the Rhymes

In a glade where the sunbeams play,
Words skip merrily, come what may.
A rabbit recites in a goofy style,
While foxes roll over, laughing the while.

Amidst the giggles of leaves so bright,
Chasing shadows, they dance in delight.
With each little verse, our spirits renew,
In nature's embrace, we're silly too.

The Lush Landscape of Language

In fields of rhyme, I lost my way,
Words tangle like vines in bright array.
I tripped on a pun, and oh what a fall,
Hilarity sprouted; I couldn't recall.

Commas danced like leaves in the breeze,
Periods hid behind flowering trees.
Metaphors sprouted with playful zest,
Each line a jest, and I was their guest.

Echoes of a Verdant Verse

In the forest of phrases, I took a stroll,
Found a couplet that wanted my soul.
It giggled and wiggled, what a fine sight,
I laughed so hard, it turned day into night.

A stanza burst forth with a chuckling sigh,
It wandered around with a flicker and fly.
I caught it, you see, in a jar made of rhyme,
But it broke free, seeking more humorous time.

Pining for the Perfect Phrase

I yearned for a line to tickle my mind,
Searching the chapbook, but none I could find.
Then a word jumped out, looking quite bold,
It winked and it danced, oh the stories it told!

With laughter I chased it through syllable skies,
Where each phrase erupted in whimsical sighs.
I finally caught it, my happiness soared,
But the phrase just giggled then promptly ignored.

A Muse in Every Leaf

Under the trees, where the muses reside,
Each leaf held a line, a joke to confide.
I plucked a haiku, it tittered with glee,
Its rhythm was catchy; it danced like a flea.

Whispers of laughter through branches did sway,
As sonnets would tumble down pathways of play.
A quatrain appeared, with a belly so round,
And we all laughed aloud at the joy that we found.

Whispers of the Cedar Glade

In the glade where whispers play,
The trees gossip night and day.
With leaves like curtains, they conspire,
To spread tall tales that never tire.

Squirrels in tuxedos, oh so spry,
Debating acorns under the sky.
A debate that's loud, a chirpy shout,
While blue jays plot their daring route.

Frogs croak rhymes of lovesick woes,
While crickets strum with their fine toes.
Laughter blooms like wildflowers grown,
In the woods where silly seeds are sown.

With each rustle, a punchline waits,
Even the owls join in debates.
In the cedar's charm, all seem to meet,
A comedy show with nature's beat.

Sonnet Revival: A Forest's Embrace

Lost in a forest, a jester wanders,
His cap and bells ignite wild wonders.
Every tree's a stage, every root a base,
Where laughter blooms and frowns erase.

A hedgehog in shades critiques the jokes,
While trees giggle, adorned in cloaks.
Their wisdom found in bark and stone,
A sonnet crafted with humor shone.

Each syllable dances, each rhyme will play,
As the critters chuckle through the day.
Leaves swirl like words, brisk in the breeze,
Sharing secrets among the trees.

Thus the forest, with mirth, upholds,
A sonnet's revival, in laughter enfolds.
With every gust, we join the fun,
Celebrating verses until the sun.

The Evergreen Echo

In the echo of trees, laughter rings,
A chorus of joys that nature brings.
Pine cones tumble, making a scene,
As squirrels juggle with nuts unseen.

With every rustle, a tale unfolds,
About mischievous owls and their gold.
The bumblebees buzz a curious tune,
Around flowers painted bright as the moon.

The shadows play tricks, they dance around,
Planting chuckles within the ground.
In this lively grove, not a dull note,
Every echo's a giggle, a funny quote.

So gather, dear friends, let spirits soar,
In the evergreen whisper, come back for more.
From roots to branches, the laughter's free,
In this echoing realm, where we all agree.

Verses in the Canopy

High up in the canopy, tales take flight,
With parrot puns fluttering in delight.
Branches sway to a tree-top beat,
As chipmunks choreograph nimble feet.

Rabbits, in bow ties, share fancy chats,
While bats hang upside down, wearing hats.
Each leaf's a page in their quirky book,
Filled with mischief, if you take a look.

With blossoms laughing at old tree knots,
The forest gathers for humorous thoughts.
Under twinkling stars, the verses play,
A nighttime jest for all to stay.

So step into this leafy hall,
Where ancient woods giggle and call.
In the verses woven, fun finds a way,
With each rustle, more laughter on display.

A Canvas of Colorful Cadence

With crayons in hand, I start to create,
A rainbow of words, oh won't it be great!
My poetry's messy, splashed here and there,
A masterpiece formed with vibrant flair.

Each line is a stroke, unexpected and wild,
Like a child with a brush, oh artfully styled!
Rhymes tumble like paint, in a comical dance,
Turning serious thoughts into a silly romance.

Reimagined Reflections in Verse

I gazed in a mirror, but what did I see?
My reflection grinned back, quite humorously!
It tickled my thoughts, a sight to behold,
With verses like jokes, so carefree and bold.

I flipped through my lines, a whimsical spin,
Each stanza's a riddle where laughter begins.
In this quirky allure, truth seems rather shy,
But fun takes the stage, while wisdom waves bye!

Brushstrokes of Meaning

With brushes dipped deep in the pot of my mind,
I paint silly stories, uniquely combined.
A sprinkle of nonsense, a dash of delight,
Crafting sonnets of laughter that dance through the night.

Each stroke adds a giggle, each word, a cheer,
In this playful art, no seriousness here!
The canvas is alive with mischief and glee,
My brush scrawls a narrative for you and for me.

Serenading the Soul with Style

I serenade words in a jazzy old tune,
While squirrels in top hats dance under the moon.
My verses are parties where humor collides,
The rhyme's got some rhythm, the laughter abides.

Each stanza a jive, every line a parade,
With chuckles and giggles that never do fade.
In ludicrous style, my soul takes the lead,
Spreading joy through the verses, that's all that we need!

Rethinking the Written Word

Words can be tricky, they dance and they twirl,
I wrote down a sonnet, it gave me a swirl.
The punctuation laughed, it jumped on the page,
My grammar went wild, like a modern-day sage.

Mix metaphors here, let similes fly,
A chicken in a tux, and a cat in the sky.
Who needs structure when chaos is grand?
Let's turn the whole world into a quirky band!

Sculpting Lines in Light

Lines should be sculpted, like dough in my hands,
Every odd little thought, just like shifting sands.
I chisel a pun with a giggle and glee,
As a cactus-wearing sombrero winks back at me.

Through laughter and whimsy, my verses will glow,
An octopus tango, a walrus in tow.
Oh joy, dear muse, with your shenanigans bright,
Let's frolic through meters from morning to night!

Infinite Beauty in Rhythm

Rhythm is merry, like socks that don't match,
A duck in a bowtie, a quirky old catch.
Each beat has its style, a jig and a jive,
I rhyme with a giggle, oh how I thrive!

Let's dance with our words, a conga of rhyme,
A parrot that sings from a faraway clime.
In banter and bounces, the verses take flight,
With lyrics so funny, they shine ever bright!

Elevating Emotion Through Poetry

Emotions are tricky, like cats on a roof,
They leap into sonnets, but who's the goof?
Fluffy clouds giggle, while raindrops hum tunes,
And feelings make faces, wearing silly balloons.

A heart in a tutu, a grin on its pace,
With joy that's contagious, it joins in the race.
Through highs and through lows, let the mirth intertwine,
For poetry's magic is all about fun time!

In the Shade of Timeless Trees

Under branches wide and green,
Squirrels play their prankish scene.
Acorns fall like tiny bombs,
Nature's jest, her playful charms.

A woodpecker gives a peck,
While singing frogs arrange a wreck.
In the shade, secrets unwind,
Whispers of the playful kind.

The breeze brings laughter, soft and light,
Tickling leaves, a joyful sight.
Each rustle tells a quirky tale,
In this woodland, humor prevails.

So let's embrace this goofy spree,
Where nature's laughter sets us free.
In every leaf, a joke exists,
Amongst the trees, we can't resist.

Cadence of the Conifer

A conifer takes a daring stance,
Holding secrets with a merry dance.
Its needles whisper all day long,
Turned into a quirky song.

The pinecone's wink is rather sly,
Saying, "Come and give me a try!"
You might just find a hidden prize,
Or maybe just some pine-scented lies.

The branches wave like they can't wait,
To join the mischief at nature's gate.
With every rustle, giggles grow,
In this forest show, we steal the show.

So dance with me beneath the stars,
Let's hold hands with the moon and Mars.
For in this groove of tree and fun,
The rhythm of life has just begun.

Woodland Waltz: A Rhyme Untold

The woodland floor sings a funny tune,
Dancing critters beneath the moon.
With every step, the mushrooms sway,
In this waltz where creatures play.

A rabbit twirls with a sly little grin,
While a hedgehog joins, and spins in.
The fox, a jokester with quick feet,
Tells tales of snacks and treats to eat.

The trees all giggle, shaking their bark,
As night falls softly, deep and dark.
Pixies toss glittering light,
In this woodland, all feels right.

With each small leaf, a laugh is found,
On nature's stage, we dance around.
Join the waltz of forest glee,
In this rhyme, we all feel free.

Nature's Symphony of Sonnetry

Beneath the sky, a song is made,
With chirps and hums, a grand parade.
The frogs are crooning in the swamp,
While fireflies put on a dazzling romp.

A bumblebee buzzes a hearty beat,
As flowers sway on tiny feet.
The wind joins in with a breezy cheer,
Creating laughter that we long to hear.

The frogs wear crowns of lily pads,
Playfully strumming, wearing glad rags.
Each note floats soft in the twilight air,
Nature's humor is everywhere!

So clap your hands and tap your toes,
Join nature's band where laughter flows.
In this symphony, we all belong,
Singing sweetly, life's a song!

Nature's Stanza: A Lush Ode

In the forest where squirrels play,
Trees wear their leaves in a silly way.
A bird sings high, with a comical squawk,
While rabbits dance in whimsical flock.

Sunlight flickers, a game of chase,
A chipmunk tumbles, what a funny face!
Nature's rhythm, a jolly tune,
Under the laughter of a bright full moon.

Harmonies of the Ancient Pine

Oh, ancient pine, with branches wide,
What secrets in your needles hide?
A squirrel giggles, lost in your maze,
While the wind jokes in rustling rays.

You sway with grace, yet sometimes crook,
A wise old tree with a storybook.
The sun peeks through, a golden grin,
Even the shadows dance and spin.

The Refreshing Brush of Green

In the meadow, greens play tricks,
A playful kitten pounces, then skips.
Blades of grass tickle tiny toes,
While daisies wink at the bright blue shows.

The breeze whispers jokes, oh what a tease,
As butterflies twirl in the afternoon breeze.
A picnic spread with treats galore,
And ants think they're at a buffet store!

Lyrical Leaves in Spring's Caress

Leaves burst forth in a vibrant cheer,
Each one dances, bringing good cheer.
A toad croaks at a passing fly,
While the blossoms wink and shy.

Breezes laugh, tickling the blooms,
As nature plays, the garden zooms.
A chubby bumblebee joins in the song,
Buzzing joyfully, all day long.

The Metamorphosis of Meter

When the feet start to dance, oh what a sight,
Verses whirl and twirl, pure delight!
Iambs trip over each other, quite a mess,
But laughter erupts, who could care less?

Dactyls skip along, a merry parade,
While spondees look grumpy, their fun has been frayed.
Anapests bounce, giggling full of cheer,
While blank verse just sulks; it's stuck in a sphere.

Free verse joins in, a wild, reckless mate,
With shapes so bizarre, oh, isn't it great?
Poetic chaos reigns like a jest,
And rhyme just giggles, "I'm the very best!"

So let's play with words, twist them around,
In this merry dance, our joy can be found.
With verses so silly, they're bound to amuse,
Turn your sonnets silly; it's what we all choose!

Gilded Imagery in Quatrains

Gold-plated sunsets, who knew they could rhyme?
Clouds dressed in jewels, looking oh so sublime.
A chicken in top hat struts 'neath the moon,
While trees play the trumpet—a whimsical tune!

Birds flash like diamonds, with spats and a show,
They argue in quatrains, putting on quite a glow.
Ducklings recite lines, with flair they perform,
While fish in the pond debate in a swarm.

Gilded canaries sing sonnets of fish,
Their wishes for freedom, each one a small wish.
As lilies in tutus do pirouettes there,
Who knew that such flora would join in the fare?

With laughter and imagery weaving through air,
A garden of quatrains—joy we all share.
Let whimsy run wild; it's the key to delight,
In this quirky world, everything feels right!

Elegance Woven in Rhyme

In a world made of lace, where verses take flight,
Rhyme drapes like a gown, sparkly and bright.
A cat in a tutu prances with grace,
While cupcakes hold court in this fancy space.

A snail in a top hat discusses haute cuisine,
With whispers of buttercream, sugar, and sheen.
While spiders spin sonnets, their webs interlace,
Crafting fine patterns, a delicate trace.

The frogs in their bow ties belch lines full of flair,
As daisies throw petals, all floating in air.
With every sweet line, elegance blooms,
In this whimsical world, creativity looms.

So let's frolic in rhyme, take a leap and a bound,
In this garden of laughter, let joy be our sound.
With verses so charming, we twirl through the night,
In elegance woven, our spirits take flight!

Transcendent Themes Emerging

Through questions of cheese and the meaning of wine,
We ponder the cosmos—oh, isn't it fine?
With cupcakes as planets and sprinkles in space,
Each theme finds its rhythm, a laugh-filled embrace.

A squirrel in a tuxedo debates life's great quests,
While butterflies flutter to put minds to rest.
"I'm transcending my dreams," says a pie in the sky,
As creamy delights give metaphors a try.

The shadows of pickles dance under the moon,
With cucumbers spinning to a most festive tune.
In this realm of absurdity, wisdom takes flight,
As laughter and nonsense blend perfectly right.

So let's muse on our muses in this witty play,
With whimsical themes guiding us on our way.
In laughter there's meaning, in folly, we dive,
Transcendent in jest, we flourish and thrive!

Intricate Layers of Expression

In the garden of words, I plant with glee,
Each pun a seed, sprouting humor for free.
Stanzas wiggle, giggle, dance with delight,
Verbs wear bright hats, a funny sight!

Metaphors prance, twirling like a clown,
While similes slip in, wearing a frown.
Rhyme schemes tumble, like cats in a chase,
In this word playground, there's joy to embrace.

Puns bounce about like a rubber ball,
Each twist and turn, we're having a ball.
Laughter cascades like a waterfall's flow,
Join in the fun, let your humor show!

With layers so rich, like a cake made of cream,
Verse serves a slice, fulfilling a dream.
So come take a bite, savor each line,
In this lyrical feast, there's no need to dine.

Rhythmic Revelations

Dancing with rhythm, my lines take a stroll,
Feet tapping in time, like a jazz-loving soul.
Words shimmy and shake, partners in crime,
Chasing the beat, like a jolly old rhyme.

Shock and surprise sprinkle laughter like confetti,
My verses all jive, neither frumpy nor petty.
With punchlines that leap, they fly through the air,
Making you chuckle, without a single care.

Meter skips lightly, a hopscotch delight,
Each stanza's a giggle, a tickle for light.
Chords of the heart strum a silly sweet tune,
Under the sun, or beneath the bright moon.

Let's paint with our laughs, a mural so grand,
With every tickle, we'll make a new brand.
Time to rejoice in the playful delight,
As we groove and we sway, through day and through night.

New Echoes in Familiar Frames

In frames of old, new echoes resound,
Whispers of laughter, a joy that's profound.
Tickling fancies with echoes from past,
Words leap off the page, oh, what a blast!

The clock may be ticking, but humor won't fade,
In corners of poems, funny creatures parade.
Old metaphors dance with costumes so bright,
Inviting the reader to join in the fright.

Shadows reveal silly faces so clear,
As laughter erupts, it's music we hear.
With rhythms that wobble and phrases that grin,
A chorus of chuckles where silliness wins.

Painted in colors of jokes we all love,
Each stanza's a gift, like a warm hug from above.
In familiar frames, let the laughter ignite,
With echoes that shimmer, we take flight tonight.

The Rebirth of the Lyrical Landscape

In the landscape of words, a renewal's begun,
Silly horizons are stretching for fun.
Hills of humor rise, with valleys of cheer,
And every verse echoes, 'Come one, come here!'

Flowers of puns bloom in fields of bright rhyme,
Tickling the senses, a joy so sublime.
Each phrase takes a leap, like a frog on a spree,
Let's bounce through the lines, wild and fancy-free.

Trees of tall metaphors sway in delight,
Casting shadows of laughter, both playful and light.
While clouds of confusion drift high in the sky,
We'll pluck funny fruits, just you and I.

With the sun shining down, it's a perfect scene,
A rebirth of laughter, colorful and keen.
So let's roam this landscape, where giggles abound,
In this lyrical garden, pure joy can be found.

Rhymes Refined with Intention

In a land where the words take flight,
The poets gather, oh what a sight!
With quills in hand and hats askew,
They dance around, oh yes, it's true.

A rhyme is penned, but oh dear me,
A banana slipped—what chaos, whee!
Verses tumble, laughter in the air,
Who knew that poetry could be such a dare?

With puns galore and winks to spare,
Each line's a jest, light as a hair.
They rhyme of cats with a penchant for cheese,
And giggle at the words that come with ease.

In this merry hall of wordy fun,
The sonnets shine like the midday sun.
So raise a glass and toast the jest,
For laughter, my friends, is truly the best!

The Curated Collection of Craft

A shelf of poems neatly aligned,
With titles quirky, oh how they shine!
Who wrote the sonnet about a duck?
Of course, it's crafted, just pure luck.

Each line a puzzle, a playful tease,
Crafted to fit like a tailored breeze.
With winks and nudges, the poets play,
Turning dull afternoons into a ballet.

The words jump round, like frogs they leap,
Over metaphors, they'll take a sweep.
So grab a pen and join the spree,
Let your laughter ring, come write with me!

And when you've penned a piece so fine,
Remember a giggle is just divine.
In the curated world of silly rhyme,
Every line's a jest, a spark of time!

Daring Explorations in Expression

Into the wild of words we dive,
With a net of humor, we will thrive.
Each phrase a riddle, each joke a key,
Unlocking laughter, oh joyous spree!

With daring leaps, the rhymes abound,
In fields of giggles, we twirl around.
A rhyming cow, a dreaming hen,
Who knew this madness could spark such zen?

In the realm of wit, boldness reigned,\nWith every pun,
more sanity drained.
But fear not, dear poets, let's ride the wave,
A dash of humor will surely save!

So grab your pens, and don't hold back,
In this lively journey, we'll find our track.
With giggles and grins, let's break all molds,
In expressions daring, let laughter unfold!

Melodies in Metre

In a world where rhythms reign,
A sock may dance, quite insane!
With mismatched shoes and hats askew,
We laugh aloud, it's fun and new.

The cat may croon a tune so loud,
While the dog jumps, oh, so proud!
In quirky beats our hearts align,
Laughing together, we feel divine.

A jumbled line, a whimsical rhyme,
Turning daily chores to silly mime.
With friends so dear and jokes that flow,
Each moment sparks a joyful glow.

So let's embrace this rhythmic spree,
With laughter shared, we feel so free!
In quirky verse, we find our beat,
Life's a melody, oh so sweet!

Reviving the Classic Stanza

Oh, the olden times we try to bide,
With quills and ink we cannot hide.
Yet here we sit with coffee cups,
And poetry that really erupts!

A sonnet gone astray, you'll see,
With squirrels debating jubilee.
In lines like jigs, we twist and spin,
Creating canvases of grin!

Each stanza holds a secret flair,
Like penguins in a fancy pair.
With metaphors both wild and spry,
We tread on pages, oh, my oh my!

So pen a verse, and raise your glass,
To playful words that humorously pass!
For every rhyme can shape a smile,
Let's bask in giggles for a while!

Graceful Gatherings of Words

Gather 'round, you clever folks,
Let's mix our metaphors with jokes!
A garden of laughter, wild and free,
Where daisies dance and giggle with glee.

Words like candy on our tongues,
With puns that jingle like old songs.
The trees will listen, nod, and sway,
As we twist and turn in playful play.

In the shadows where giggles bloom,
We craft our lines in a joyful room.
With echoes of laughter, the magic's done,
A gathering of words like a secret pun!

So raise your pens and spread the cheer,
For every line, let's shed a tear!
With joyous hearts and minds that whirl,
In this wordy dance, we twirl and twirl!

Chords of Creativity

In the symphony of silly schemes,
Our thoughts take flight like wacky dreams.
With laughter strummed on hope's guitar,
We weave our tales, oh, so bizarre!

Creativity flows like sugarplum rain,
As we juggle words, what a delightful pain!
With puddles of ink and paper boats,
We set sail to dance with our quotes.

In chaotic harmony, we find our tune,
With spoons and sporks, we'll dance by the moon!
As scribbles turn to symphonic dust,
We create chaos, it's a must!

So join the fun, get in the groove,
With every word, let's make our move!
Together we'll laugh and bravely create,
In this whimsical world, we celebrate!

A Tapestry of Tenderness

In a garden of rhymes, a gnome pranced,
Wearing socks with sandals, he danced.
His hat was too big, it flew like a kite,
Chasing thoughts like bubbles, what a sight!

A hedgehog recited with great delight,
His quills all askew, a humorous fright.
Birds critiqued each line with a chirp,
While the sun took a break and began to burp.

A frog wrote sonnets from a lily pad,
Bemoaning his luck, for despite being rad,
He leaped to conclusions, a splash was his fate,
Rhymes fell like rain while he tried to relate.

So gather your verses and let laughter gleam,
In this tapestry woven, a hilarious dream.
With every mishap, share your charm,
For in poetry's dance, we disarm!

Crafting the Sublime

A poet sat down with a cup of tea,
Determined to pen lines that were carefree.
But a cat on the desk knocked his papers about,
And now he has prose that he won't talk about!

His muse turned to mischief, a squirrel with flair,
It juggled the verses, threw walnuts in air.
Each rhyme got a twist, and each line took a dive,
What once made sense now barely survived.

The haikus went wild, turned into large pies,
As rascal raccoons plotted under the skies.
They sang in a chorus with bowls set ablaze,
Making sure his sublime was simply a maze.

In the end, he laughed, what a racket of fun,
With mismatched stanzas all coming undone.
So craft your own chaos; let the laughter fly,
For a joyful sonnet can make spirits high!

Varied Voices in Verse

Beneath a leafy tree, a chorus did form,
Each creature with verses, delightful and warm.
The turtle was slow, with rhymes like molasses,
While the rabbit would race, making time for his classes.

A parrot chimed in with a voice oh so shrill,
Repeating the lines that would give you a thrill.
"Polly wants a rhyme!" she squawked with a grin,
As a fish in a pond tried to jump in the din.

So a snail penned a rhyme that was bound to be gold,
But it took him an hour, or so he was told.
With every creation, a laugh and a cheer,
In this varied assembly, no one shed a tear.

Unique in their rhythms, they sang with delight,
As the sun set on stages, their verses took flight.
So gather your voices and let stories merge,
In the heart of the laugh, let the fun always surge!

Fabled Fragments Rediscovered

In a dusty old attic, a book of lost lore,
Filled with tales of brave knights and a dragon who snore.
But the pages were stuck, with honey and jam,
Oh dear, what a sticky predicament—blam!

A princess who dreamed of a glamorous chance,
Lost her shoe in a whimsical dance.
While a fairy with sass tried to fix up her curls,
But was tripped by a knight's clumsy whirls.

Explorers returned with maps drawn in crayon,
Fabled fragments lost all their place from the spawn.
Each twist of the tale, a giggle to share,
As characters tangled in knots of despair.

Now in the moonlight, they laugh and they play,
Rediscovering fragments in a jumbled array.
So keep up the quest for stories untold,
For in every misstep, great laughter unfolds!

Rhapsody of the Rooted Realm

In the garden, weeds hold court,
Dancing wildly, a greenish sport.
Bugs in bow ties approach the fruit,
While squirrels conduct a nutty suit.

Flowers giggle in vibrant hues,
Whispering secrets, sharing news.
The trees claps to the bumblebee,
As laughter flows like honeyed tea.

Rabbits argue over carrot pies,
Planting dreams beneath the skies.
Nature's choir sings off-key,
Each note a jest, bright jubilee.

Behold the fun in tangled roots,
A symphony of veggies' toots.
In this realm, the light is low,
Where humor grows, like a wild show.

Twilight's Embrace: Poetry in Shadows

As evening falls, the shadows play,
Poets trip in a word ballet.
Ghostly lines dance on the page,
While owls coo at a midnight stage.

Moonlight spills like milk on grass,
Humor glows, none can surpass.
The crickets chirp their little jokes,
A symphony of leggy folks.

Wit weaves through the night like thread,
As fireflies scatter, light you read.
Under the stars where laughter lives,
Each verse a jape that nature gives.

In twilight's arms, we dream and scheme,
With goofy smiles, we start to beam.
For shadows may seem rather grim,
But in them, all the jokes begin.

The Sonnet's Soul in Scenic Splendor

In fields where words take flight and roam,
Funny phrases find their home.
A sonnet giggles, sways, and prances,
Each line a chance for jolly glances.

With puns that tickle and tease the ear,
Metaphors that smile, and lend a cheer.
Nature's stage, where laughter blooms,
In sunny spots and shady rooms.

Sonnet trees with trunks of rhyme,
Flourishing in a jolly time.
Scribbled thoughts like birds on wing,
Winging humor in a lively spring.

The roots of jest in poetic glee,
Where every verse is meant to be free.
In scenic splendor, let us parade,
For laughter's dance should never fade.

Illuminated Lines Beneath the Foliage

Beneath the leaves, the lines grow bright,
Illuminated with sheer delight.
Each verdant twist a quip awaits,
As nature's jester gleefully creates.

A pumpkin grins, all orange and round,
While vines do pirouettes on the ground.
Frogs in tuxedos croak a tune,
As fireflies join a waltzing moon.

Wordy critters playing with cheer,
Crafting sonnets we long to hear.
The roll of laughter spills from trees,
On breezes sweet as summer's tease.

Under the canopy's leafy smart,
Each line's a beat in the poetry's heart.
In this green haven, life's a jest,
Orchestrated by nature, and simply the best.

Meditations in the Swaying Branches

When trees begin to dance, oh me, oh my,
Their branches stretch and sway, oh where do they fly?
I tried to join their frolic, with style and grace,
But landed in a tangle, a most awkward place.

The squirrels laugh and chatter, a raucous cheer,
As I untwist my limbs, oh dear, oh dear!
Maybe I should stick to poetry's sweet sway,
And leave the fancy footwork for the birds at play.

The breeze sings softly, a whimsical tune,
While I contemplate rhymes under the glowing moon.
A sonnet in the branches, with laughter entwined,
Words float like confetti, so beautifully unconfined.

So here I sit with pen, a jest in my heart,
Creating verses silly, that never fall apart.
For in the swaying branches, where laughter is free,
I've discovered grand wisdom: just let it be me.

Reciting Rhyme Among the Pines

In deep, green groves where echoes reside,
I spout clever couplets, my fragile pride.
The pines couldn't care; they stand tall and hushed,
While I dance with my poetry and laughter is rushed.

With every word I utter, the squirrels snicker,
As I weave together humor that can't get slicker.
I ponder the moonlight as it drapes the trees,
But puns about bark have brought me to my knees.

"Ode to the Oak!" I declare in a stage voice,
But the pines roll their needles, "Do you have a choice?"
For my rhymes aim to tease yet find little grace,
Instead, they cause giggles that light up the place.

Yet gathered round the trunks, a merry crowd,
Join in my rhymes, though they may be loud.
Where laughter escapes like a breeze so refined,
The forest becomes home to the joy intertwined.

The Art of Aerial Verses

On branches up high, I try to compose,
A symphony of sonnets with a tickled nose.
But balance is tricky, I wobble and sway,
As I laugh at my efforts to rhyme and to play.

I clutch my notepad tightly, oh what a sight,
While the robins caw loudly, "You're not quite right!"
Yet their chirps turn to cheers, and I'm lifted anew,
As they dance around me, a poetic crew.

I fling a few verses, and they whirl through air,
Each line tumbles and tumbles, quite free and quite rare.
With giggles and grins, they bounce off the trees,
My aerial antics bring everyone to tease.

So here's to the stanzas that fumble and flop,
Elevated by joy in this lofty rooftop.
For the art of the verse, airborne like a kite,
In this whimsical world, I feel truly light.

Whispers of Refined Rhyme

The pines are the listeners, tall and serene,
As I whisper my rhymes, so rare and so keen.
With each gentle rustle, I hear their delight,
In a poetry party under soft moonlight.

I tiptoe through verses, careful and sly,
While the owls peek down with a questioning eye.
"Is that a rhyme about pancakes and rain?"
They blink and they hoot, their feathers to feign.

A soft breeze carries giggles, across the fair glade,
While I wax and I wane, in this sonnet parade.
The trees can't stop laughing, their wisdom so bright,
As each little stanza takes off in mid-flight.

So hug the tall trunks and sway with the breeze,
Let humor find roots, and don't take it with ease.
For the whispers in rhyme are the heart of the fun,
And the night laughs along till the rising sun.

A Symphony of Syllables

Silly sounds and jumbled dreams,
A poet's play, or so it seems.
With every phrase a playful dance,
Words prance around in a merry chance.

The cat looked up, and so did the dog,
They joined the fun, in a loving fog.
A twisty rhyme, a ticklish beat,
Laughter spins on poetic feet.

In cups of tea and pies of fruit,
Verses wear their best, oh so cute!
With giggles nestled in each line,
They tickle hearts, oh how divine!

So come and join this silly spree,
Wrap verses like a warm-up spree.
In every laugh, a gift we find,
This symphony is sweet and kind.

Verses Adorned with Grace

In a garden bright, words bloom and sway,
Dresses of phrases twirl and play.
With petals soft and colors bold,
Each line a story ready to be told.

A monkey sings, a frog does prance,
In this dance of words, we take a chance.
Fluffy clouds and giggly trees,
Capture joy in verses with ease.

Hats on flowers, what a sight!
Rhyme and rhythm, pure delight.
With blushing blooms and playful stakes,
Watch the humor as laughter breaks.

Verses twirl in a dazzling trance,
A whimsical world, so full of chance.
With each giggle and loving embrace,
This funny dance adorns with grace.

Radiance in Rhymes

A starry night with verses bright,
Glowing words take their flight.
With winks and blinks, they dance and play,
Radiant joy, they simply sway.

A turtle jogs, a snail takes flight,
Under the moon's soft, glowing light.
They sing of fun, a merry tune,
With giggles ripple like a balloon.

Sunshine sprinkle in every line,
Each verse wrapped in laughter, so fine.
With silly grins and sparkly eyes,
This joyful dance makes spirits rise.

So gather round, let laughter chime,
In this magic of rhythm and rhyme.
With radiant hearts, we adopt the climb,
In this festival of words, sublime.

Finesse in Every Line

In every line, a twist of flair,
Poetic pranks float in the air.
A juggling fish, a polka-dot mouse,
Whirling around in a playful house.

With a leap and a bound, the words take flight,
Chasing the moon through the starry night.
A hat on a cat, a bow on a bee,
Dancing with rhythm, so wild and free.

Scribbles whirling like candy floss,
Giggling echoes, they're never at loss.
With a wink and a grin, they take their bow,
Finesse in every rhyme, oh wow!

So let's embrace this whimsy spree,
Sing aloud of joy, you and me.
With finesse and fun, our hearts align,
In every chuckle, we brightly shine!

Unveiling Verses in New Light

Once upon a poet's plight,
Words tangled in a fright.
With each scribbled line, a dance,
Forget the rules, take a chance!

Rhymes tumble like a clumsy cat,
Chasing after dreams and chat.
Chortles echo in the night,
Verses giggle with delight!

Stanzas waltz like wild balloons,
Inflated by silly tunes.
Let your misspellings be bold,
A comic tale yet untold!

Lines may wobble, bend, and sway,
But laughter's here to stay!
In this sonnet, joy's the aim,
And poets earn their silly fame!

Flourish of Feelings on the Page

Feelings blossom, bud, and bloom,
In a garden full of gloom.
As I write, the flowers giggle,
Mixing laughter with a wiggle!

Sunshine tickles every phrase,
Making grumpy lines ablaze.
The bees buzz jokes in every turn,
While stubborn rhymes begin to churn!

A daisy dressed in polka-dots,
Swaying to the laugh's sweet knots.
Words prance, wiggle, and express,
A playful form of wordy mess!

Twirling thoughts on grassy blades,
Where hefty doubts gently fade.
In this garden, let's be free,
And sip on verses meant for glee!

The Resurgence of Refined Verse

In suits and ties, the verses dress,
But wait, what's this? A comic mess!
They strut and boast, but trip and fall,
A fancy ball becomes a brawl!

With monocles and silly quirks,
These refined lines, oh how it works!
They poke and prod with clever glee,
Who knew that sonnets could be free?

Polished words that laugh and tease,
In tuxedos, they never freeze.
Their charm a knot of silly glee,
At this grand gala, come and see!

A waltz of wit amidst the prose,
Elegant echoes, who needs those?
In this dance of poet's plight,
Laughter wins by sheer delight!

Transformative Tones in Poetry

Tones evolve like chameleons,
Dancing with their silly genes.
From grumps to giggles, all things switch,
Transforming lines from grumpy to rich!

Words do flips; they tumble down,
While laughter wears the funniest crown.
Beneath the surface, joy ignites,
In subtle hints of youthful fights!

Chirpy chirps and goofy grins,
Make dullish phrases wear some fins.
Poetry is a silly game,
Where every tone's both wild and tame!

So let us play with words so bright,
And turn the heavy into light.
In this realm, we're all absurd,
Where nonsense sings and laughter's heard!

Breathing Life into Stanzas

A poem once sighed, felt quite bland,
With rhymes that tangled like a rubber band.
It yearned for some spice, a touch of delight,
So it danced with a frog in the pale moonlight.

Metaphors sprouted, growing quite tall,
Like weeds in a garden, they laughed at the fall.
With puns in the air, and laughter just right,
This poem now bubbles with joy, what a sight!

An ode to the chaos, a playful affair,
Where verses bounce high, like kids without care.
It juggles and tumbles, a circus in rhyme,
Each line tickles fancies, oh what a fine time!

So here's to the laughter, the joy in each word,
May your verses be silly, absurdly absurd.
Let the sonnet parade with a wink and a grin,
As poetry dances, let the fun begin!

Sentiments Shrouded in Foliage

Amidst twisted branches, the lines sneer and play,
Leaves whisper secrets—come join the bouquet.
Each word takes a tumble, a twirl in the breeze,
Silly squirrels giggle, mischief with ease.

A flower's a pun, a thorn's just a jest,
In this leafy realm, laughter's the quest.
Petals of humor flutter in a whirl,
Colorful chaos dances, a whimsical swirl.

Sentiments tangled, a tree's leafy braid,
Voices emerge from the shade as they wade.
The fruit of this folly hangs ripe on the vine,
Taste laughter and joy in each wording divine!

So come join this garden, don't wander alone,
For silliness grows where the wild seeds are sown.
With branches that sway, under skies bright and clear,
Let poems enshroud us with laughter and cheer!

The Refreshment of Rhythmic Roots

Roots tangled and knotted, oh what a sight,
They giggle, they wiggle, in dance of delight.
A rhythm emerges, all bouncy and spry,
As verses take flight, like a bird in the sky.

Each beat is a tickle, a tick and a tock,
With a hop, skip, and jump, like a playful rock.
Who knew these old roots had moves like a star?
Doing the twist while reciting from afar?

The soil chuckles softly, a whisper of cheer,
As poems emerge with a chuckle and sneer.
From dirt comes the laughter, and joy fully bloomed,
In gardens of giggles where all muses loom.

So let's praise the rhythm, the roots' funny dance,
With a wink and a nod, let your sonnets entrance.
With laughter as water, and glee as the light,
We'll refresh every line, till the shadows feel bright!

Elysian Verses Among the Pines

In forests of laughter where verses align,
Pines sway to sonnets, a symphonic design.
They giggle in breezes, tossing words in delight,
A symphony crafted by day and by night.

Among needles and cones, odd rhymes bounce and play,
Squirrels recite puns, while walkers delay.
With echoes of poetry, laughter takes flight,
A chorus of giggles in the soft, muted light.

Oh, what a scene, verses tickling each other,
Line feeds off line like sister and brother!
The humor they weave, it's a playful disguise,
As pine trees roll laughter beneath starry skies.

So wander these woods, let your worries unwind,
Among elysian verses, true joy you will find.
With nature to guide, and puns so divine,
You'll leave with a smile, and your heart will align!

Fresh Takes on Timeless Themes

In a garden where rhymes grow,
A squirrel dances, stealing the show.
With acorns he juggles, not a leaf in sight,
He laughs at poems that can't take flight.

Old sonnets dressed in threads of gold,
Try to keep up, but they feel quite old.
A chicken in boots joins the fun parade,
As classic lines get a wacky upgrade.

With metaphors spinning like tops in a breeze,
And similes dancing like bees in the leaves.
The sonnets chuckle at their outdated charms,
While wordplay runs wild through the poetic farms.

So gather your lines, and twist them all about,
Let laughter burst forth, give a joyful shout.
For poetry's feast is a bright buffet,
Where humor sprinkles joy in a quirky way!

Lyrical Makeovers

Once a sonnet sat, quite stern in its chair,
Donning a frown, in despair and despair.
But a makeover squad came with style and cheer,
With glitter and laughter, the mood brightened here.

They teased out the lines, made them sassy and bold,
With jests and giggles, those rhymes turned to gold.
The iambs were tickled, the verses went wild,
A cheeky old sonnet became quite the child.

Now sported in colors of vibrant delight,
It dances through pages under moonlight.
No gloom on its face, just a grin ear to ear,
As it skips merrily, shedding its fear.

So join the revamp, let your sonnets play,
Inject some mischief in their lyrical sway.
A little fresh spin can turn dull into bright,
And laughter will echo through the poem tonight!

Stanzas of Renewal

In a world where stanzas can tire and grow stale,
A quick little twist sends them right down the trail.
A turtle in sunglasses, a hat on its head,
Recites witty verses while lounging in bed.

The old lines are stretching, craving fresh meat,
They giggle and wiggle, just itching to greet.
With fresh paint and polish, they come back to life,
No longer a sonnet filled with old strife.

An octopus pens lines with eight fancy pens,
While juggling some rhyme schemes and crafting new trends.
Each stanza a story, each laugh quite sincere,
As spry little rhymes bloom, spreading good cheer.

So breathe in new life, give those words a spin,
Let flairs dance and twirl, let the good times begin.
For every old form needs a cheeky, fresh start,
To blossom and tickle the poetic heart!

Polishing the Poetic Gems

A diamond of a sonnet lay under some dust,
Its lines all tangled, not a whisper of trust.
Then came a young bard with a grin wide and bright,
With laughter like magic, he polished by night.

He rubbed off the grime with a twist of a line,
And lo! That old sonnet began to shine.
Each quatrain erupted in quirky delight,
As metaphors shimmered, all giddy and light.

With playful puns dancing around in a swirl,
The old words grew lively, all twirled in a whirl.
As laughter arose from each polished phrase,
The gems sparkled boldly with fancier ways.

So if your old verses are looking quite flat,
Just give them a tickle and a playful spat.
For poetry's magic can brighten the scene,
With humor and joy making all things serene!

Crafting Elegance in Verse

In a world where rhymes take flight,
I tripped while trying, what a sight!
Puns and giggles, words on the loose,
My elegant art, a playful noose.

With each awkward phrase, I cleverly dance,
On the edge of chaos, I take my chance.
A sonnet's a party, come join the fun,
Just mind the punchline or you'll be undone!

My quill is a wand, I'll cast a spell,
Words like confetti, oh what the hell!
In this whimsical world, don't be too shy,
Twist the pot like a poet gone awry.

So let's laugh and play with meter and rhyme,
Making verses that tickle, oh so sublime.
For in every line, a chuckle does wait,
Crafting elegance, it's never too late!

The Art of Elevated Lines

With every syllable, I reach for the sky,
But my ladder is wobbly, oh my, oh my!
I pen lofty thoughts, quite the endeavor,
Yet my muse trips over words, clever as ever.

Lines that soar, but then they plunge,
Riddled with giggles, oh, how they lunge!
I wield my pen like a sword in fun,
Battling syntax, but who's really won?

An elevated thought, a pun for the day,
A twirl of pure laughter, in my own way.
With lofty ambitions, I aim to delight,
But watch as my humor takes off in flight.

In the art of the line, let joy freely flow,
A rhythm of chuckles, a whimsical show.
With verses as bouncy as a trampoline,
Who knew writing could be so serene?

Harmonies in Stanza

In stanzas we gather, a merry crew,
With harmonies tangled, what shall we do?
A chorus of laughter, a symphony bright,
As verses collide in the dead of night.

Let's march to a rhythm, out of sync with grace,
Painting our sonnets, a comical space.
With every heartbeat, a chuckle is born,
In the land of the scribes, new tales are sworn.

A cauldron of jests, I stir with delight,
But somehow the words just took wing, what a sight!
Harmonize mayhem, welcome to the stage,
As echoing laughter breaks out of its cage!

So let's sing our stanzas, a jovial tune,
With words that dance, like a buffoon.
For in the sweet chaos, a magic is spun,
With harmonies bright, let us all have fun!

Resplendent Words in Twilight

As twilight descends, my quill brings a flare,
With words calmly glowing, let's not despair.
Resplendent in meaning, yet goofy at heart,
With each stroke of ink, I give humor a start.

From the shadows of dusk, laughter ignites,
In the magic of stanzas, where mischief delights.
Crafting my sonnets with dazzling intent,
But lo and behold, what a quirky event!

So grab a fine drink as the moon takes its place,
Let's scribble some wonders, affixed with a grace.
In twilight's embrace, playful whispers flow,
As resplendent words become part of the show.

With chuckles unbounded and joy all around,
In the realm of the funny, new gems can be found.
So toast to the twilight, where laughter does swell,
In the glow of our verses, let's bid all farewell!

A Journey Through Refined Lines

In a land where rhymes take flight,
Even squirrels recite with delight.
A poet juggles words with glee,
Where verses dance like leaves from a tree.

A sonnet slips upon a shoe,
It trips and laughs, as poets do.
With each quill stitch, a chuckle spills,
Crafting lines that give us thrills.

One line winks, another one nods,
They play tag, like mischievous gods.
A rhyme jumps high, a meter falls flat,
In this sonnet garden, how about that?

So let your words take a whimsical whirl,
In a world where laughter can twirl.
A journey through refined, silly schemes,
Where every stanza bursts with dreams.

Essence of Emotion in Elegant Phrasing

Oh, the essence of feelings we dive,
With giant pins, we try to survive.
Words painted bright, though some may smudge,
A slip of the tongue can make us judge.

Heartstrings plucked by a feathered quill,
Emotions dance as we giggle still.
A teardrop glimmers, a grin appears,
In this ballad of chuckles and cheers.

Metaphors wear socks that don't quite match,
Imagery funnier than a comedy sketch.
With laughter echoing off each line,
A paradox wrapped in verses so fine.

Emotions swirl in a humorous pitch,
Where joy and sorrow make a rich niche.
So join the fun and embrace the thrill,
Of elegant phrasing that gives us chill.

The Dance of the Inspired Pen

Watch the pen as it twirls with zest,
Crafting phrases that are simply the best.
It pirouettes over paper's wide stage,
Creating giggles, unleashing a rage!

With each stroke, it jiggles and shakes,
Inventing puns and all sorts of fakes.
A waltz of words, both silly and grand,
Laughing at rhymes all over the land.

A limerick joins with a somber tale,
Spinning round like a derailed snail.
In this dance, joy never ends,
As the inspired pen leads us, my friends!

So grab a pen and join the fun,
It dances on paper until it's done.
With words that jive and rhythms that play,
Let's shimmy with joy, come what may!

Rediscovering Poetic Pathways

In pathways where rhymes go astray,
We find silly signs that lead us each day.
A poet lost, with a map upside down,
Exploring the folly in wordsmith's town.

Each step we take, a chuckle unfolds,
Where metaphors bloom like flowers in gold.
A joke whispers softly, 'Oh, look over there!'
Where sonnets skip, and laughter fills air.

The road is bumpy, with stanzas galore,
Some cleverly crafted, while others ignore.
Yet in this adventure of whimsical fate,
We discover our voices, and it's never too late.

So wander these paths with a joyful embrace,
Find humor in lines, leave behind the chase.
Rediscovering poetry's silly delights,
As we dance on the page through grace and giggles bright.

Resplendent Reflections

In a mirror, I see a clown,
With a frown that turns upside down.
Shiny shoes and a big red nose,
Who knew laughter could strike a pose?

Reflective giggles fill the air,
As silly faces dance with flair.
A playful wink, a cheeky grin,
Life's too short, let the fun begin!

Playful Phrasing and Poise

Words flip like pancakes on a grill,
Some stick, others slide with thrill.
Jokes and jests weave through the night,
Crafting laughter until their flight.

In a sonnet, puns take flight,
Twisting meanings, oh what a sight!
Hiccups of humor burst and bloom,
Chasing away the shivers of gloom.

Enchanting the Everyday

Each morning's toast can sing a tune,
With butter spread like a sunny moon.
Jelly swirls in a joyful dance,
Who knew breakfast could take a chance?

From mundane chores, we find the thrill,
A laundry sock could promise a thrill.
Dancing brooms and giggling mops,
In the ordinary, joy never stops.

Metaphors in Bloom

The daisies wear tiny top hats,
While butterflies lead fancy chats.
Metaphors spring like flowers anew,
In the garden where giggles grew.

Life's a circus, come join the show,
With juggling dreams and a cheeky glow.
Laughter blooms brighter than the sun,
In the land of fun, we're never done!

Renewing the Poetic Palette

Oh, my quill has taken a dive,
In a pool of ink, it fights to thrive.
A splash of humor, a twist of wit,
Let's paint the lines with a giggle fit.

With stanzas bright and rhythms spry,
I'll rhyme like a squirrel, jump and fly.
The verses bounce like a rubber ball,
In this poetic game, I'm having a ball!

Words dance like flames in a silly jig,
Each couplet sings, but don't call it big.
The laughter spills from each crafted line,
As I chuckle along with my sparkling rhyme.

So grab your pen, give it a whirl,
Let's turn the mundane into a swirl.
With joy in our hearts and laughter, too,
Let's create a world where nonsense is true!

A Dance of Words and Whimsy

In a garden of letters, where giggles grow,
I twirl with the vowels, putting on a show.
With consonants clapping and commas that cheer,
This whimsical waltz brings us laughter, oh dear!

Each stanza hops like a bunny on joy,
Playing leapfrog with whimsy, oh boy!
I skip through the syllables, light on my feet,
In this dance of delight, can't accept defeat!

The adjectives twirl in a whirlwind of fun,
Adverbs pirouette, and the rhymes all run.
With playful puns as the guests of delight,
The verses all laugh till the morning light.

So grab your rhyme shoes, let's head for a spin,
In this circus of language, let the fun begin!
We'll bounce on the beats, with a chuckle so bright,
In a dance of wordplay that lasts through the night!

Lines of Clarity and Charm

With a wink and a nod, I write down my thoughts,
In lines so clear, they tie up the knots.
A jiggle of laughter, a sprinkle of cheer,
These words won't break, they'll just bend and leer.

Rhyme like a kid who's just found a toy,
Let's mix up the verses, oh what a ploy!
Humor's the glue that binds us today,
In this lyrical playground, let's romp and play.

With metaphors naked, I giggle with glee,
As I conjure up visions that tickle and tease.
Each line a delight, a charming surprise,
A jester of language, under sunny skies.

So dance with the rhythm, let laughter be loud,
In this joyous occasion, let's gather a crowd.
With clarity shining, and charm on display,
We'll pen a delight that just won't decay!

The Quintessence of Expression

Oh, words are like candy, so sweet and bright,
Each phrase a delight, a whimsical bite.
With metaphors tickling my fancy with glee,
I craft a collection pretty as can be.

Verses are jigsaw pieces that fit just right,
A puzzle of laughter, oh what a sight!
With humor and joy dancing through the air,
These lines weave a story, beyond compare.

Lines leaping like kittens in playful delight,
I capture the essence of whimsy tonight.
Each stanza a chuckle, a grin on the page,
In this illustrated world, I shine like a sage.

So come, take a seat, let's savor the fun,
In this theater of words, we've only begun.
With a sprinkle of laughter and joy in our hands,
We'll pen the quintessence that forever stands!

Serene Structures of Expression

In a garden of words, a seed is sown,
Where rhymes dance around like a jester's tone.
A pun here and there, a chuckle ignites,
Even Shakespeare might giggle at our plights.

Meter's a mess, but who really cares?
We'll throw in some laughter, the joy that it shares.
With every odd couple, a smile appears,
Crafting joy from the chaos, despite all the sneers.

Verses like jelly, they wobble and sway,
Each line a delight, come join the ballet.
Twirling with humor, we'll tickle the page,
As we pen out our thoughts, just let them engage.

So gather your quill, let's have some fun,
With sonnets that sparkle, never to shun.
In this world of wordplay, no rules to abide,
We'll laugh and create, let our passions collide!

Illuminating Shadows of Meaning

Oh, shadows of meaning, so vague and unclear,
They stretch with a giggle, they quiver with cheer.
Each syllable shapes, a curious plight,
What's hidden in laughter, shines ever so bright.

When meanings get twisted, we'll play with the jest,
Like tangled up yarn in a cat's little quest.
Metaphors leap, like frogs on a log,
Finding fun in the fog, it's a poetic slog.

Within every meaning, let puns take the throne,
A crown made of giggles, in verses we hone.
Beneath every shadow, a chuckle may bloom,
Causing critics to ponder and stare in the gloom.

Let's dance with the light; we'll brighten the dim,
With humor our lanterns, let's carelessly swim.
In a pool of words, let our laughter resound,
As meanings emerge from the silly profound!

Fresh Facets of Familiarity

Familiarity breeds, a poke and a tease,
With freshly baked sonnets that tickle and please.
We'll rehash old tales, in a comical twist,
Where every cliché gets a bright, cheeky twist.

Like socks gone mismatched, or shoes on the wrong,
We'll cozy in comfort, and sing a new song.
Each facet a gem, with a glimmer of cheer,
Turning boredom to laughter, it's perfectly clear.

From mundane to magic, with just a few lines,
We'll tiptoe on humor, like playful designs.
The ordinary sparkles, a riotous spree,
As familiar ghosts ride on giggles carefree.

So come join the madness, no seriousness here,
With lines that are silly, let's fill up with cheer.
In the world of the words, we'll find our delight,
With familiar old faces glowing ever so bright!

The Gift of New Beginnings in Poetry

A new dawn is rising, where laughter takes flight,
With beginnings so catchy, they feel just so right.
Each line is a present, all wrapped up in cheer,
A gift of pure joy that's now drawing near.

We'll open our verses with giggles galore,
As words tumble out and keep asking for more.
Each rhyme is a buddy, each stanza a pal,
In the fun of creation, we'll never be dull.

Let's craft something quirky to lighten the load,
A journey through laughter, wherever we go.
With rhymes so outrageous, they bounce off the walls,
New beginnings in laughter, where joy never stalls.

So dance with the muses, let whimsy take lead,
In this playful adventure, we'll plant every seed.
With every fresh start, there's a chuckle or two,
Words that sparkle and grin, all waiting for you!

Celestial Currents in Verse

In the sky where rhymes collide,
Stars dance with a comical glide.
Words tumble in a Jupiter spin,
Giggles echo, let the fun begin.

Planets hum in their own weird tune,
As meteors burst like balloons.
Comet tails tickle the moon's cheek,
Funny verses, come take a peek.

Revising Realms of Rhyme

In a land where poetry plays,
Witty lines form a hilarious maze.
Rabbits hop with quills in hand,
Edits made as they take a stand.

Nonsense rules this vibrant sphere,
Where puns and giggles abound here.
Even the trees crack a joke,
As laughter through their branches broke.

The Innovation of Imagination on Paper

Crayons scribble in a joyful spree,
Ink spills secrets of glee and esprit.
Doodles leap off the page with grace,
Tickling minds in this lively space.

Ideas bloom like flowers in spring,
Whispering tales that make us sing.
Silly thoughts set the world ablaze,
As imagination dances and sways.

Finessed Flourishes of Feelings

Emotions flip like a pancake stack,
With syrupy laughs that keep us on track.
Joy leaps from the pages with flair,
As the sad faces vanish in air.

A whimsy wind nudges a rhyming kite,
Chasing clouds through day and night.
Feelings prance under the sun,
In a world where poets just have fun.

www.ingramcontent.com/pod-product-compliance
Lightning Source LLC
Chambersburg PA
CBHW051657160426
43209CB00004B/931